SEARCHING FOR THE SWEET SPOT

Dave at University Retirement

Searching for the Sweet Spot:
A Planner's Memoir

David R. (Dave) Godschalk

ISBN-13: 978-1544191157
ISBN-10: 1544191154

ACKNOWLEDGMENTS

I gratefully acknowledge the constant editorial assistance of Lallie Godschalk, whose keen memory, sharp eye, and language skills were indispensable to the writing of this account. I am deeply indebted to Jack Benjamin for his outstanding and patient technical work in restoring the flawed and dim photographs that tell more than words. Betty Hughes, Martha Hsu, and A.J. Dean helped me through the myriad technical challenges of turning my writing into book form.

In terms of the larger story, there are too many people to thank by name. Every accomplishment listed here depended on the work of colleagues and teaching and research associates. Plan making, research, and graduate education are collaborative enterprises. Their success, and the pleasure they provide, result from actively working together in team linkages.

CONTENTS

LIST OF ILLUSTRATIONS

"Ah...this here is a sweet spot, this island-- a sweet spot for a lad to get ashore on. You'll bathe, and you'll climb trees, and you'll hunt goats...Why, it makes me young again."

Long John Silver in Treasure Island by Robert Louis Stevenson

FOREWORD

During my life, I spent a lot of time searching for the "sweet spots" in work and relationships. Every activity has its own sweet spot. In tennis, hitting the ball on the racquet's sweet spot produces the most powerful shot. In city design, sweet places where people want to congregate result from optimal groupings of urban open space, buildings, and movement systems. In art, sweet paintings that make viewers want to look deeply result from ideal blends of color, shape, and emotion. In human relationships, sweet rapports result from perfect mixes of empathy, respect, and love

Thinking about sweet spots helps me understand more about who I am and how I navigated the past 85 years. My journey took me from the plains of Oklahoma to the hills of New Hampshire, from the Mediterranean Sea to the shores of Florida, and finally put me ashore in the North Carolina Piedmont. Along the way, there were many planned and unplanned sweet spots.

Both my parents and major outside events shaped my life. My mother and father, Helen and Harold Godschalk, were not "helicopter parents;" they did not hover over and direct me every day. However, they strongly influenced my critical choices. Helen convinced me to apply to Dartmouth College and Harold suggested that I become an architect. Without their guidance, my life would have been completely different.

Outside events also made huge differences. President Kennedy's recall of active Navy Reserve ships during the 1961 Berlin Crisis interrupted my family and professional plans and ultimately led me to a teaching career. The single most important event of all was a seemingly casual blind date in 1958 to attend a Robert Frost poetry reading at the University of Florida with Lallie Moore Kain, who was to become my wife and closest friend.

Design has been an abiding thread in my life. As a Dartmouth undergraduate, I designed my fraternity's party room addition and created their Winter Carnival ice sculptures. As a Navy officer, I redesigned the wardrooms for two ships. As a planning consultant and city planning director, I designed Florida urban renewal projects, neighborhoods, and downtowns.

In academia, I redesigned the format of the *American Institute of Planners Journal* during my term as editor. As a planning professor, I designed graduate education curricula, land use plan-making methods, and tools for mitigating natural hazards and building urban resilience. As chair of the Chancellor's Buildings and Grounds Committee and member of the Design Review Group, I played a central role in preparing and implementing the $2.3 billion University of North Carolina campus plan.

As a board member of Carol Woods, my retirement community, I chaired the task force that prepared the 2010 master plan for building $22 million in new apartments and facilities. Following university retirement, I designed a framework for incorporating best sustainability practices into comprehensive plans that the American Planning Association has now adopted.

As a watercolor painter, I still search for design and composition sweet spots. However, I have learned that you do not always find the sweet spot of everything from plans to paintings by design. The process is often more complicated than that.

Pictures selected from my collection highlight my story. More a collage than a detailed memoir, this graphic narrative includes images of significant people, relationships, environments, and events that fall roughly into nine sometimes-overlapping chapters. A family tree diagram at the end of this memoir depicts my immediate Oklahoma family, starting with my grandparents and proceeding to my grandchildren.

1. Oklahoma Beginnings: 1893-1931

I grew up in Enid, Oklahoma, a new town created on land bought by the federal government from the Cherokee Indians, after their forcible resettlement from North Carolina on the "Trail of Tears." This Oklahoma territory opened to settlement in 1893 with a land rush in which settlers raced with each other to stake their claims. A rough-and-ready history of competition, claim jumping, fresh starts, and aggressive town building framed its character. Laid out by the U.S. Army Corps of Engineers along the route of the Rock Island Railroad, its site previously had been part of the Cherokee Outlet leading from the tribe's reservation to their hunting grounds farther west.

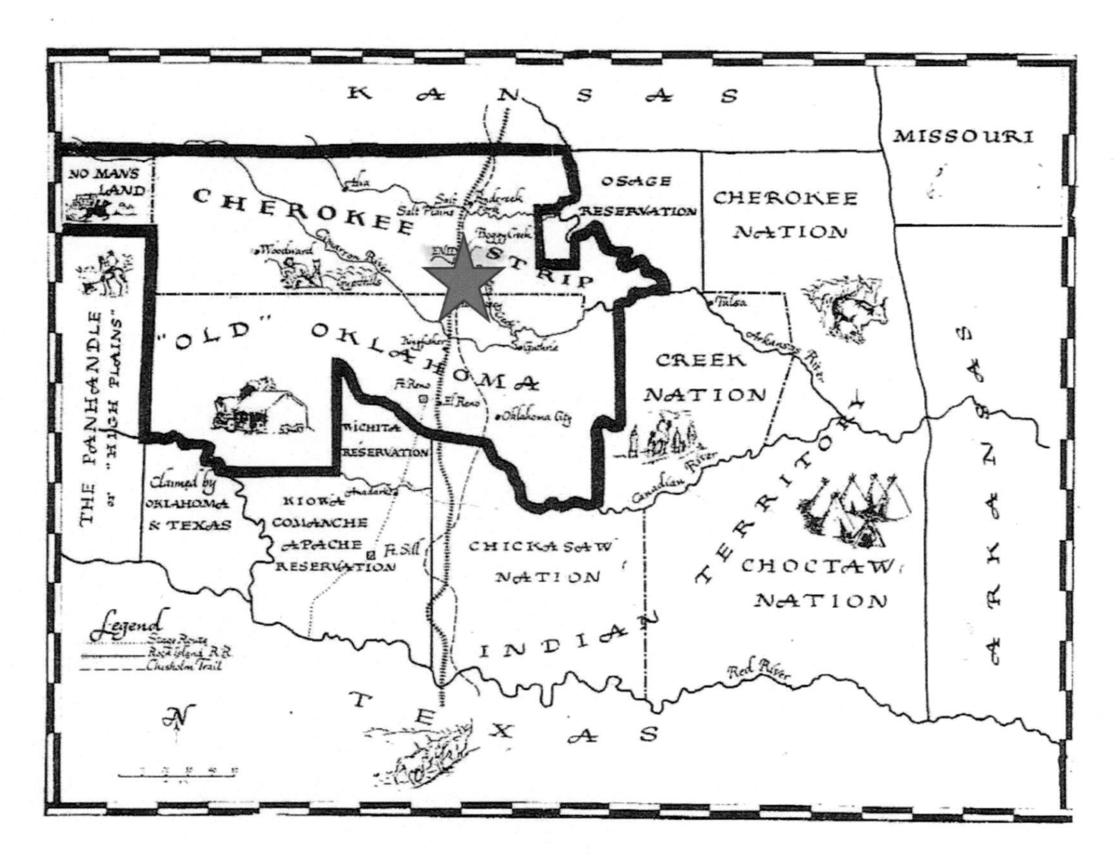

1-1. Cherokee Strip Map. Amidst Indian reservations. Showing Enid location (star) on Rock Island Railroad line. Source: The Cherokee Strip: A Tale of an Oklahoma Boyhood, by Marquis James. Norman: University of Oklahoma Press, 1945.

My 26-year old Dutch grandfather, Marinus Godschalk, joined the rush and claimed a downtown lot in Enid. He and his cousin, Joe Meibergen, had no horses, so they made the run on the train. At the time, the Rock Island railroad did not stop in Enid, intending to put its station in North Enid. Joe jumped off as the train passed through Enid, breaking his ankle. Marinus stayed on to the North Enid station and came back to find his cousin propped against a tree, and then proceeded to claim their lot. They went on to establish the Meibergen and Godschalk men's clothing store, selling Hart Schaffner and Marx suits to pioneer settlers.

1-2. Meibergen and Godschalk Store. Marinus Godschalk (on right).

Later, Marinus bought his cousin out, took over the store, and became one of Enid's leading businessmen. In a 1937 Works Projects interview for the Oklahoma Indian-Pioneer history project, Marinus recalled that most of the pioneer men wore ordinary clothes, and that five-gallon hats were rare. To establish their business, Meibergen and Godschalk traded clothes for firewood and took out ads in the local paper selling the advantages of ready-made suits.

KICKERS

Are numerous. The army mule--the overloaded shotgun and the ballet girl are all great kickers. But they're not in it with an able-bodied man when he once gets wound up. He gets a pass to a show and he kicks. ..He goes to a first class hotel, sits down to a first class meal, and begins to kick...Clothes kickers are

ESPECIALLY

unreasonable. They'll go to a swell tailor, and stand on a dunce block for twenty minutes to get measured—wait a week over time for a suit—and if it doesn't fit just so—then let the tailor fit it over. Let the same man walk into a clothing store, and he kicks before he is hardly in...He knows nobody can fit him, knows this, that and the other. But he saw a suit that a friend bought here and if he can get a fit like that---! You are especially

INVITED

fellow kickers, to come in and kick. You're URGED to come in and try on things. You're urged to come in and find fault with things. We've got some suits that we think are perfect—and we'd like you to see them. You know that HERE you can try on a suit and SEE if it fits. If it doesn't, you can try on another. At a tailor's you can't do that. You buy it FIRST, and TRY it afterwards—maybe it fits—maybe it doesn't—but you take it all the same. We are yours anxious to please.

MEIBERGEN & GODSCHALK, THE LEADING CLOTHIERS

The disagreement over where the railroad would stop stemmed from the fact that the North Enid site selected by the railroad was located on Indian land allotments while the government selected its town site for Enid three miles further south. The Rock Island refused to stop or even slow down at the Enid site. In 1894, Marinus and other Enid business leaders forced the railroad to move its station in Enid by sawing through supports of its trestle bridge and wrecking the train. They used a crosscut saw that hung in Marinus's garage for many years.

1-3. Wreck of Rock Island Freight Train 1894. Twelve cars went off the track. Source: "O County Faces and Places: A Collection of Cherokee Strip Photographs and Stories." 1968.

Marinus grew up near Assen in the northeastern Netherlands. An entrepreneurial young man, he emigrated to the U.S. at the age of 20 to work for an uncle in Cawker City, Kansas. After resettling to Enid and starting his business in 1893, he persuaded his childhood sweetheart, Bertha Trompetter, to come to America and marry him. She traveled alone by ship to New York and by train to Cawker City, where they were married in 1895. She remembered the cowboys firing their pistols outside on their wedding night. Their daughter Sara was born in 1896 and their son Harold in 1898.

1-4. Marinus Godschalk

1-5. Bertha Godschalk

My mother's parents, Oscar Robinson and his wife, Nannie West, grew up near Alexandria, Tennessee. After their wedding in 1903, they moved to Oklahoma, first to Woodward, then to Ft. Supply, and then to Gage where Oscar managed a lumberyard. Their daughter, Helen Faye, was born in 1904 and their son, James Clifford, was born in 1906. Nannie remembered Oscar getting their first car in 1918, but she never learned to drive. The family moved to Enid in 1920, where Oscar became an independent grain dealer. He regularly visited the local farms and grain elevators, and kept his grain samples in little cloth bags in a big roll-top desk in his office in the bank building

1-6. Oscar and Nannie Robinson

Although raised in Enid, my parents could have chosen to live elsewhere. They both went east for further educational opportunities, Mother to Emerson College of Dramatic Arts in Boston and Dad to Columbia University in New York City. Mother considered trying for a stage career but decided to come back to her family home and marry Dad. He studied journalism, which became his career, and geology, which did not pan out when Marinus sold his oil leases after a drilling accident. In the end, she settled for the Junior Welfare Follies and he became managing editor of the *Enid News and Eagle.*

1-7. Helen Robinson at Emerson College   *1-8. Harold Godschalk 1928*

Harold Godschalk and Helen Robinson were married in Enid in 1928. Their marriage proposal was controversial. Her Scotch-Irish, Presbyterian Tennessee parents, Nannie and Oscar Robinson, were opposed to their daughter marrying into the Dutch Jewish Godschalk family. Even though Bertha and Marinus did not observe religious practices, their heritage was clearly visible in a small, primarily Protestant, Oklahoma community. However, love triumphed.

1-9. Helen Godschalk as Bride

2. An Enid Boyhood: 1931-1949

Helen and Harold settled into a house on West Cherokee Street about equidistant between their parents' houses, where I was born in 1931. Both sets of grandparents helped to look after me, although I spent more time with Oscar, who took me with him on his rounds to farms and grain elevators. He introduced me to the locations of small town life, including his office with its roll-top desk in the bank building, the stores fronting the town square, the small civil airport, and the Rock Island Railroad station, where the engineers would recognize him with a whistle toot. Five years later, my brother Dick was born and we built a new house at 1320 West Wabash Street in the original Enid suburb, the Kisner Addition.

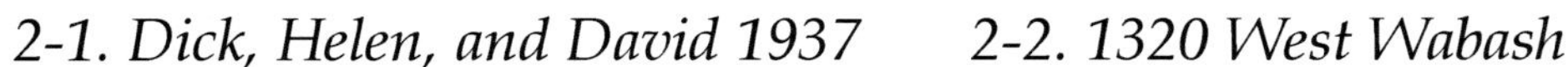

2-1. Dick, Helen, and David 1937

2-2. 1320 West Wabash

That suburban neighborhood, with its nearby elementary school and other young families with children, became the location of all of my boyhood friendships and adventures. It was the ideal layout for free roaming kids, adjacent to wheat fields and within hiking distance of Boggy Creek. Taft elementary school, hosting a diverse mix of poor rural and middle-class suburban kids, was just a few blocks from our house. Since this was the pre-television and pre-digital era, radio programs and cowboy movies were my main source of commercial entertainment. Every afternoon after school I listened to "The Green Hornet" and "Jack Armstrong: All American Boy." Every Saturday I attended a double-feature western movie where we competed to win the most applause for our cowboy outfits. Believing that David was too formal, I began to call myself "Dave." I had to wrestle my friend, Bob Barnes, to the ground to convince him to use my new name.

2-3. Taft School 6th Grade. Bob Barnes (3rd from left in first row, Dan Sours and Dean Reed (2nd & 3rd from left in second row, Dave (1st in third row)

Our extended family got together for holidays, birthdays, and casual suppers. Dad's sister Sarah had married a local attorney, Roy Elam. Since all three branches of the Godschalk, Robinson, and Elam families lived in Enid, I regularly visited my grandparents, uncles and aunts, and cousins. It seemed normal to know all three generations of relatives.

2-4. *Godschalk, Robinson, and Elam Families*

After a disagreement with the publisher (who reneged on a partnership agreement), Dad left the newspaper and joined his father in the Godschalk clothing store on the Square in downtown Enid. Dad was an able but reluctant clothing merchant. His family persuaded him to join the family business with the idea of preserving it for Dick and me. However, after Marinus died in 1942 and WWII made customers scarce and stock difficult to get, Dad declared bankruptcy and went out of business in 1944. I remember the tearful family dinner when he finally told Mother about it. The store was a relic. It still had traces of its old history, including tin ceilings and an oiled wooden floor.

During World War II, the Air Force built Vance Field, a training base, in Enid. Like other families, we took in a boarder. A World War I veteran, Dad was too old for the military; he took a job with the U.S. Office of Price Administration in Oklahoma City. After the war, he started a new career as director of advertising and public relations with the Failing Supply Company, a brainchild of George Failing, who had invented the truck-mounted drilling rig for oil exploration. Given his newspaper experience, writing facility, and photographic skill, Dad was a natural at this. While not an avid sportsman, he liked to fish and was proud of landing a big tarpon during a fishing trip on the Gulf of Mexico.

2-5. Harold- Failing's Advertising Director *2-6. Harold with Tarpon*

As a boy, I went everywhere on my bike, going to grade school and junior high, and then to downtown for the Saturday cowboy movies and a drugstore lunch with Dad. The Second World War brought gasoline rationing but the salesman father of my friend Dean Reed had gas for a panel truck. Our teen-age group spent many evenings cruising around the drug stores looking for something to happen and listening to The Hillbilly Hit Parade on the truck radio. After the war, Dean and I bought an old 1931 Oldsmobile, cut the top open, and used it to transport our cronies.

2-7. Dave and Dick on Back Porch *2-8. Our "Merry Oldsmobile"*

My teenage interests were a mix of drawing cartoons, building gasoline-powered model airplanes, and playing sports. Summer activities included swimming the Country Club pool, mowing lawns and washing cars at local filling stations. I was a camper and then a counselor at the YMCA camp in the Arbuckle Mountains.

2-9. Challenger Model Plane *2-10. Diving at Country Club*

In high school, I lettered in football and edited the yearbook, a pattern of straddling divergent camps of jocks and intellectuals that carried forward the rest of my life. A better editor than football player, I was blindsided on the first defensive play of my junior year and sat out the season with a dislocated elbow. Senior year went better with no major injuries and interesting football friendships with teammates, some of whom were military veterans.

2-11. Guard on Enid High Football Team 1948

My steady girlfriend was Kay Lou Francisco, Queen of the May in our senior year. Teenage social life involved escorting her to high school dances and parties, many put on by the DD or Dirty Dozen, an old Enid social club dating back to the town's early days. Always looking for dramatic touches, I borrowed Mother's make up kit to add a rakish mustache for the DD gangster party. My inherited early interest in theater would follow me into college.

2-12. Escorting Kay Lou, May Queen 1949 *2-13. DD Gangster Party*

By the time of my graduation from high school, my mother and father had already influenced my future life. Dad gave me an interest in words, writing, and editing, as well as steering me toward architecture. He called on the architect who designed our Enid house to explain what architects did and to describe his practice to me. Mother gave me an interest in applying to Dartmouth College and exploring the wider world. She told me stories of attending Winter Carnival while at Emerson College, as the date of a Dartmouth student. When the Navy awarded me an NROTC fellowship, I put Dartmouth as my first choice and the University of Oklahoma, where Kay Lou and most of my friends were going, as my second choice. To my surprise, Dartmouth accepted me and I set off for the unknown territory of New England.

3. AN OKIE AT DARTMOUTH: 1949-1953

Flying to Boston on my way to Hanover, New Hampshire, marked my first commercial airline flight and my first venture east of the Mississippi River. My childhood friend Bob Barnes, on his way to MIT, left Enid with me and we never moved back. At the Boston airport, it took forever to decipher the cab driver's thick accent. Traveling up to Hanover on the Boston and Maine Railroad was like entering a foreign country. The only person I knew in Hanover was John Talley, a junior and the son of an Enid doctor. He became a lifeline in a strange sea of preppies, seminars, freezing winters, and overturned expectations about Dartmouth life, along the way taking me down to Boston for an Old Howard burlesque show and my first pizza.

Dartmouth was a challenging new world for me. My preconceived model of campus life was similar to that of Yale and Princeton, with students socializing with martinis and wearing flannels and tweeds to class. However, instead of formal cocktail parties and rep ties, social life was beer in the basement bar and class wear was jeans and flannel shirts. Isolated in the north woods, the school prided itself on its macho image and back to nature persona. The nearest female companionship was at Colby

Junior College, thirty some miles away. After my effortless Enid high school educational experience, I was jolted by professors who expected their mostly prep school graduates to have mastered the arts of class discussions and weekly paper assignments. It was an intellectual stretch and an eye-opening adjustment.

After getting a "D" on my first English theme, I learned to amuse my instructor with stories from small town Oklahoma life. While not sophisticated in Shakespeare, I was an expert in Saturday night around the Enid town square when the farmers came to town in their pickup trucks. Tales from Midwestern wheat and oil country made surprisingly good themes.

My dormitory was another shock. A bare-bones structure of concrete block walls and Spartan rooms, Topliff Hall was reminiscent of public housing. However, my fellow inmates there--John Shaddock, Wade Sherwood, Fred Niles, and Len Johnson--became lifelong friends. I went to Bermuda for spring break with Fred, was best man at John's wedding in Denver, became engaged to Len's sister Thora, and cruised the Greek Isles with Wade years after we graduated. However, that first year, I missed Oklahoma, Kay Lou, and my old friends from Enid. I tentatively explored with the NROTC Commandant the possibility of transferring back to the University of Oklahoma. He convinced me to hold off on a decision until after my summer midshipman cruise, by which time I had acclimated to the wilds of New Hampshire.

3-1. Bermuda Spring Break 1951

Dartmouth redirected my career plans, leading me to a new vocation. Entering Dartmouth, I thought I was interested in following in my father's footsteps into an advertising career. Two Dartmouth professors, Hugh Morrison and H. Wentworth Eldredge, convinced me instead to take a Modified Art major that combined architecture and city planning—then a new and little known profession. Fortunately, for my intellectual and professional development, this major included hands-on courses in architectural design as well as art and architectural history. This began my understanding of the central role of design as the key driver of urban planning. As I took courses in that major, I began to find my way at Dartmouth.

As a freshman, I explored a number of new activities. Still somewhat stage-struck, I landed a role as a kid in a play by Frank Gilroy, an older student who graduated to a successful career as a playwright, authoring "The Subject Was Roses" and other Broadway productions. I auditioned for a slot as an announcer on the college radio station, where my Oklahoma twang qualified me instead as a western music disk jockey. My program, Western

Styles in Music, would run for four years playing the western swing of Bob Wills and the workingman's ballads of Pete Seeger long before country became cool. Fred Niles talked me into trying out for freshman lacrosse, where it quickly became evident that we did not stand a chance against the Deerfield and Groton graduates.

3-2. The Kid in Gilroy's "The Great Art." (Dave far right)

My sophomore year was much more successful. I pledged Phi Delta Theta, gained an active social life, dated Thora Johnson from Colby Junior College, and made more close friends--Fred Chase, Dick Blum, and Mayo Johnson from my fraternity; Bert Melcher, a gregarious westerner whose Cadillac transported us to and from Hanover; and Pete Grenquist, a fellow NROTC midshipman with a wicked sense of humor . My fraternity brothers nicknamed me "Okie" and kidded me about my competing Dartmouth and Oklahoma girlfriend pulls.

3-3. *Phi Delt Pledge Class 1950*

3-4. *Okie Caricature*

Dartmouth increasingly looked like the place for me. Art and design became central interests and I did some watercolor painting with Paul Sample, the artist in residence. I designed a basement party room and Winter Carnival ice sculptures for my fraternity.

3-5. *Dave and Thora at Winter Carnival*

During an Enid visit after my junior year midshipman cruise, I discovered a hard truth about the pitfalls of going home again. Cocky from recent personal successes and a few beers, I went with Ray Davis and Dean Reed to a local dance in the nearby town of Fairview. The crowd of hostile harvest hands there quickly identified us as unwelcome city boys. Insults began to fly. Before we figured out that we were in deep trouble, I found myself squared off in a fight with the local champion. Unlike Tom Cruise in *An Officer and a Gentleman,* I had never mastered self-defense. By the time Ray pulled my opponent off me, I had a black eye and a broken nose.

By my Dartmouth senior year, the long span of art history and city building began to make sense to me. I did well in my courses, made Phi Beta Kappa and graduated with honors. Despite not being a spit and polish midshipman, the Navy appointed me as commandant of the NROTC battalion. My skiing improved enough to let me think I could try to move from the Hanover golf course to the dauntingly steep headwall at Tuckerman's Ravine with my Phi Delt brothers Mayo Johnson, Fred Chase, and Dick Blum. That was an overreach. I crashed there on my final college downhill run during a spring overnight trip, breaking my wooden ski but luckily not any bones.

3-6. Dave and Mayo at Tuckerman's Ravine 1953

Back in Enid, things were moving along. Dad, an entrepreneur like his father, broke into the radio business. Through contacts in Washington, he managed to win a competitive license to operate a new local radio station. With financing from his Enid friends, he put KGWA (960 AM) on the air. Not only did he include regular programming, but he also set Mother up with her own daily talk show, The Talk of the Town, broadcasting from the spare bedroom in our house on West Wabash. Her naturally friendly personality was perfect for the show, and she got many call-ins from local listeners, ranging from housewifes to truck drivers. Meanwhile, my brother Dick and his friends made their own fun, riding freight trains out to local towns and "borrowing" Oscar's car for unauthorized evening jaunts.

3-7. Helen's "Talk of the Town"

However, tragedy struck in 1952, when Mother received a diagnosis of lung cancer. George Failing paid her expenses to fly to Mass General in Boston for treatment where she underwent radical surgery in the fall, with apparent success. However, as with other family crises, my parents were not forthcoming about the critical nature of her illness. She and Dad put on a good face when I visited her in Boston, but she was unable to withstand the side effects of the follow-up chemotherapy. When I came back to Enid for the holidays and visited her in the hospital, I was shocked to find that she was already dying. She came home from the hospital for Christmas but died shortly after. Her death tore up our family; she was the glue holding us together. We were totally bereft.

Although she had been the reason that I went to Dartmouth, sadly Mother did not get to see me graduate in June 1953. Dad came to Hanover, as did mother's cousin, Thelma Elliott and her husband Arthur, from Corpus Christi, Texas. President Eisenhower was the featured speaker, delivering his famous caution about burning books, a rebuke to Senator McCarthy and his Communist witch-hunting. Dad was more impressed that Ike admonished us to "have a little fun every day." My roommates, Blos and Mayo, said farewell. I received my regular Navy commission as an Ensign and packed up for my next move--to sea, leaving up in the air my college enthusiasms, including the status of my relationship with Thora.

3-8. Blos, Mayo, and Dave at Graduation 1953

4. CRUISING THE MEDITERRANEAN: 1953-1956

Luckily, the Navy gave me a choice active duty assignment on the heavy cruiser, USS Des Moines (CA 134). Homeported in Norfolk, Virginia, she served as a rotating flagship for the Admiral of the Sixth Fleet in the Mediterranean. Within a few weeks of graduation, I was standing on the Acropolis in Athens, site of the Erechtheum temple, the subject of my senior thesis at Dartmouth.

4-1. Ensign Godschalk USN   *4-2. USS Des Moines CA 134*

For three wonderful years, I explored the art, architecture, and cities of Europe, inspecting the ruins at Baalbek and the sculpture at the Uffizi. I visited my Dutch cousin Vera and her family in Assen in the Netherlands and skied the Matterhorn. That bachelor freedom convinced me that I was not ready for marriage; regretfully I broke off my engagement to Thora.

Navy life suited me. We young officers competed to be the best at our jobs, from decoding signals to controlling combat air patrols. My billets included Signals Officer, Combat Information Center Officer, Officer of the Deck Underway, and Public Information Officer. My men and I worked well together. I relished ship handling, even the high stress night maneuvers to turn a 20-ship task force into the wind for carrier takeoffs. My PIO duties brought me into contact with newspaper reporters in our ports, who took me for drinks after work, and I edited the ship's cruise book. The other young officers were great companions, both at sea and ashore. My superior officers had confidence in me. They promoted me and sent me to advanced night air control training in Key West, where my class flew to Havana for our graduation picnic. As a twenty-something year old, I could not have had a better mixture of leadership experience, comradeship, fun, and responsibility.

4-3. CIC Officer

Our ports of call ranged from Naples to Barcelona and every place in between. Our Med homeport was Villefranche, a colorful seaside village between Nice and Monaco. The Des Moines was popular everywhere. As soon as we anchored at Villefranche, the ship was surrounded by boatloads of the sailors' local girlfriends.

When we visited Beirut, we would be entertained on the fantail by belly dancers and other performers from the Kit Kat Club, a local nightclub reputedly owned in part by the Sixth Fleet Admiral. In every port, local citizens invited us for dinners and dances. The fleet was supposedly there to keep the Mediterranean safe from the Russians while the Korean War was raging on the other side of the globe, but the process of showing the flag made for wonderful tourism.

4-4. Kit Kat Club Dancer

After a couple of serious years touring all of the historic cities and architectural sites of Europe, I was ready to join a rollicking social group of junior officers who called themselves the Animal Club and focused on partying in the clubs and bars of the Mediterranean. Those friendships that I made on the Des Moines persisted: Jack McDermott, Jim Watkins, Fred Way, and Warren Shine. We have gotten together in reunions in New York City, Grand Rapids, Chapel Hill, Jackson Hole, and Santa Fe to tell and retell stories from our seagoing days, while our wives and companions roll their eyes. Between bouts of sea stories, we have hiked, played tennis, gone rafting, visited museums, watched whales, and sampled the local bistros.

4-5. Animal Club Reunion, Jackson WY 2006. Lallie & Dave, Fred & Aggie Way, Carol & Lytel Baird, Jean & Jack McDermott, Janet & Jim Watkins

At the end of my three-year active duty commitment, I faced the choice of staying on in the Navy or returning to civilian life to study architecture and city planning. With some reluctance, I hung up my Navy uniform and looked for a graduate school. Harvard and Berkeley accepted me, as did Frank Lloyd Wright's Taliesin workshop. Concerned about becoming a pallid copy of a dominant genius, I turned down Wright's workshop, a contractual apprenticeship requiring menial work in his drafting room and garden. To get ready for my design education, I decided to spend a summer in Florida building houses in Fort Lauderdale with a contractor from my Enid days. That decision proved fateful. For the next six years, I would study, marry, live, and work in the Sunshine State.

5. BECOMING A FLORIDIAN: 1956-1961

While working as a carpenter in Fort Lauderdale with Sours Construction, I heard good things about the architecture and planning program at the University of Florida in Gainesville. Unlike Harvard, Florida offered to let me study architecture and planning together in one integrated program rather in separate degree programs, which convinced me to enroll. As it turned out, I ended up with only an architecture degree and some planning courses. Just before I arrived, the lone Florida planning professor had decamped to Europe to escape the John's Commission, a state senator's witch-hunt for gay faculty members. Still, this turned out to be a decisive juncture in my life, both personally and professionally.

5-1. Carpenter with Sours Construction 1956

In hindsight, not going to graduate school at Harvard was a good thing. It saved me from their rigid planning curriculum, with its focus on economics and governance, where I would have been very unhappy. (I have since learned from his biography that Harvard flunked out Frank Gehry in 1956 when he tried to introduce architectural design into his city planning project.) It allowed me to study architectural design and urban planning as two sides of the same coin—a combination that stayed with me throughout my career. My professors encouraged me to look for the sweet spots in both large and small projects. Ed McClure, a teaching assistant who taught the planning courses, would play an important role in my future professional life.

In Gainesville, I joined forces with Fred Chase, my Dartmouth fraternity brother, who had enrolled in the University of Florida Law School after a stint in the Marine Corps. In addition to my architecture courses, I had time for optional Art Department courses in watercolor painting and welded metal sculpture. Fred taught me the rudiments of bachelor cooking and came for a visit in Enid to meet my family. For campus recreation, we played tennis, a sport I would enjoy until 1996 when repercussions from a construction accident in 1956 became serious enough to require back surgery.

5-2. Fred, Dick, Dave, Enid 1956

5-3. Playing Tennis Gainesville

Between bouts of studying, Fred and I lived and partied together for the next three years, taking off on weekends to sail the Gulf of Mexico on Fred's converted Greek sponge boat. After our first year in an apartment, we rented and renovated a small house with a couple of art students and created an outdoor garden complete with a pond. Having our own house greatly increased our social opportunities.

The biggest thing that happened to me in Gainesville was a blind date with Lallie Moore Kain to attend a Robert Frost poetry reading in 1958. Lallie was in graduate school finishing an English degree. She was a member of the Tri Delta sorority, the same as my mother. We had fun bringing together our fellow students from the English, Art, and Architecture departments in limbo parties and getting in costume for the Beaux Arts Ball. It became clear that we enjoyed the same things in life and shared many values and aspirations, and that we might be an exciting life team. At the time, I did not begin to understand how much strength and pleasure I would derive from her constant love and support over the next five plus decades.

5-4. Beaux Arts Ball 1958

5-5. Lallie Moore Kain

Lallie and I became engaged in 1958. Our wedding took place in her hometown of Bradenton under the aegis of her mother, Lallie Moore Kain (later christened "Honey" by our son, David). Dad, Roberta, and Nannie came from Enid. Fred Chase was our best man and the wedding party included my brother, Dick, Lallie's cousin, Ginno, and her husband, Les Neumeister, and friends from Lallie's Tri Delta sorority, my architecture class, and my new job in Tampa. Fred Chase famously, and wrongly, opined that our marriage would not last more than six months.

5-6. Lallie as Bride 1959 5-7. Lallie, Honey, and Roberta at Wedding

For her wedding present, I gave Lallie an interest in a fish camp—a one room house on stilts a mile offshore in the Gulf of Mexico. We used Fred Chase's riverside dock as our shore base. The camp could sleep 12 friendly people on a weekend and was the site of many wonderful gatherings. Lallie took a teaching job in Tampa and used her salary to buy an outboard boat for water skiing and trips back and forth to the fish camp. We named this 15-foot MFG fiberglass craft "Olé." It would become a long-term family recreational resource.

5-8. Fish Camp Gulf of Mexico *5-9. Skipper of the Olé*

After graduation, I hoped to work in Sarasota with a leading modern architect, such as Paul Rudolph or Victor Lundy, and to design cities as well as buildings. Both offered me jobs, contingent on getting some future commissions. I passed the weeklong Florida architectural registration exam but was destined never to practice architecture. While waiting for Rudolph and Lundy, I took a job with Smith and Kennedy, a firm of architects and planners in Tampa, where I soon discovered that my main interests and talents lay with the broader urban design scope of city planning, sketching renovated city squares rather than drafting the details of architecture. Shortly after I arrived, Milo Smith created a separate planning consulting firm, Milo Smith and Associates, and made me Vice President. Bill Lynch, one of my fellow Florida architecture students, joined us and we renovated an old downtown building for our office.

5-10. Milo and Bill Tampa 1960

5-11. Winter Haven CBD Sketch

Thanks to Milo's influence and social connections, we got consulting contracts to prepare plans for many small Florida towns, under the federally supported "701" planning program. We also prepared the first two urban renewal projects in Florida—the Maryland Avenue residential project and the Tampa Riverfront mixed use project. It was a heady time to be an urban designer.

5-12. Maryland Avenue Model   *5-13. Riverfront Renewal*

My father and brother also had some big events during this period. Dick graduated from Dartmouth and received his commission as an ensign in the Navy in 1958. To our surprise, Dad showed up at Dick's graduation on his honeymoon with his new bride, the former Roberta Shaw, a widow who had moved to Enid from Oklahoma City. Roberta would be a warm and attractive companion to Dad for the rest of his life.

5-14. Harold and Roberta at Dick's Graduation 1958

6. BERLIN CRISIS RECALL; COMMITTING TO PLANNING: 1961-1967

Lallie and I bought a charming old Tampa house in a 1920's neighborhood, New Suburb Beautiful, and made plans to raise our family there. The direction of our future life seemed clear. I had competed my military service and schooling, and had become a planning consultant in private practice. I was a Naval Reserve weekend warrior on an old WWII destroyer escort, the Greenwood DE 679, moored at the St. Petersburg Yacht Club. We made friends, joined social groups, spent weekends at our fish camp, and expected to be long-term Tampa residents.

6-1. Sunset Drive House Tampa *6-2. USS Greenwood DE 679*

However, turbulence in the outside world intervened with a disruption that changed all of our assumptions. After a confrontation with Kruschev and the construction of the Berlin Wall in 1961, President Kennedy recalled the Reserve Navy ships to active duty and I found myself obligated for a year of active duty. The Greenwood was re-commissioned and Lallie and I suddenly had to rethink our barely started married life. I took leave from my firm and dug out my old Navy uniforms. Lallie took over management of the house and checkbook.

6-3. Planning for Berlin Crisis Recall 6-4. Farewell on Greenwood

Our ship did refresher training in Guantanamo Bay, Cuba, and then trained ASW (anti-submarine warfare) crews from the sonar school in Key West. Training duty in Guantanamo was colorful. After a hard day of firing and shipboard exercises, we would repair to the Officers' Club for Happy Hour drinking and relaxation. Russian submarines were active in the waters around Cuba and some nights we would get emergency calls to return from the club to our ships anchored in the Guantanamo Bay harbor. Then, stationed at General Quarters, we would race around, searching the sea with our sonars for a Red sub that had gotten into our anchorage. Amazingly, our ships never collided with each other and we even sometimes made sonar contact with an interloper

With the ship stationed in Key West, life was more regular. Lallie moved down with our boat and we rented a place across the street from the southernmost point in the U.S., with a fine view of the harbor. The Hemmingway house was just a block away. Daily life involved going out every day to sortie with a target submarine for simulated attacks by our trainee sonar crew. I came home every afternoon after work. Lallie and I water-skied and snorkeled on the weekends. All went smoothly until one fateful day when the towing cable of a passing tugboat wrapped itself around the conning tower of the submerged sub, jerking it rudely to the surface. Fortunately, our captain was a fishing buddy of our division commander and was able to make amends. Otherwise, we would have faced a court martial.

During that year of active duty, I realized that I needed to bulk up my planning background with a Master's degree. We sold the Tampa house and my stock in Milo Smith Associates, where I had not been entirely satisfied with the need to bend to the political winds, as a consultant. I applied for and received a Pittsburgh Plate Glass fellowship to support my graduate education program. After visiting Georgia Tech and Penn, I decided to enroll at the Department of City and Regional Planning at the University of North Carolina in Chapel Hill, where the Chair was Jack Parker, who I first met when he spoke to my Dartmouth course in city planning. I was encouraged by strong recommendations from Phil Steadfast, George Beardsley, and Doc Rice, other Dartmouth alumni who had chosen UNC.

The UNC Master's program was one of the top planning departments in the U.S. Founded by the remarkable trio of Jack Parker, Stuart Chapin, and Jim Webb, the Department of City and Regional Planning emphasized the practical and physical side of planning. My faculty included Ralph Gakenheimer in transportation and George Pillorge in urban design, who became both personal and professional friends. Lallie and I lived in student housing and she served as the librarian for the planning department. Thanks to Jack Parker, the faculty always included an urban designer and courses in site planning and project design. Fortunately, the UNC planning program never abandoned physical planning, despite its experiments with social planning and policy planning trends.

6-5. UNC Planning Founders: Parker, Chapin, Webb

The next 5 years solidified my commitment to city and regional planning, gave me some governmental experience, and reoriented my career from practice to academia. I completed my Master's degree, served as planning director in Gainesville, Florida, took an appointment as assistant professor at Florida State University, and returned to UNC for a PhD. Between enrolling at UNC for the Master's program and returning there for the doctoral program, we moved four times as I tried to figure out my professional future.

After graduating from UNC in 1965, a progressive reform coalition looking for a planning director to carry out their political agenda in Gainesville, Florida, recruited me. We moved back there with high hopes, expecting to forge a strong and innovative public planning program. My role model was Ed Bacon, the enormously effective architect-planner who directed the City of Philadelphia urban rebuilding program (and the only city planner featured on the cover of *Time* magazine). I wanted to follow Bacon's lead in successfully combining political support with ambitious design goals to implement significant urban design.

Once a month I swapped my planning hat for an officer's cap. When the Sixth Naval District learned that I was moving to Gainesville, they invited me to assume command of a reserve destroyer, the USS English DD 696, based in Jacksonville. Even though I was a recent Lt. Commander without command experience, my fitness reports as senior watch officer on the Greenwood during the Berlin Crisis recall must have been convincing. In addition, they needed new leadership to clean up some drinking problems within the ship's crew. I took over as English Reserve Crew skipper, weeding out the problem sailors. Under the supervision of a small active contingent, we took the ship to sea every month and to Guantanamo Bay for summer training.

6-6. USS English DD 696 *6-7. English Skipper at Gitmo*

The Gainesville appointment did not work out well. Shortly after our arrival, the two professors who masterminded the progressive group took posts at other universities, leaving our coalition without leaders and leaving me without political backers. We did some downtown design, including a parking mall for the new

Post Office, a "facelift" program for the storefronts, a proposed downtown loop road, and some zoning reform, but the progressive agenda sputtered and the old guard conservative opposition regrouped and went after the planning department. As a symbol of the new guard, my position became increasingly uncomfortable. I told Lallie "Do not finish unpacking".

6-8. Post Office Mall Gainesville 1965

The final straw came over a seemingly minor design issue in Gainesville's first shopping center. Sears, the center's developer, opposed the planning department's recommendation to move the center entrance road off the highway intersection. When I defended this on grounds of traffic safety, the local newspaper publisher told his reporters to "get me Godschalk's head on a platter." After Sears' executives flew in from Atlanta threatening to take the shopping center to another town, my planning board chair wilted. Shortly afterward, Ed McClure called inviting me to join him in creating a graduate planning degree program at Florida State University in Tallahassee. It was an easy decision. In retrospect, taking the Gainesville job turned out to be one of the best mistakes I ever made—redirecting me into the academic life for which I was best suited.

We enjoyed life in Tallahassee. As an assistant FSU professor, I taught courses and designed the Master's degree course curriculum, finding that I liked teaching and research. Lallie and I did a Ford Foundation study of the impacts of the space program at Cape Canaveral and spent six weeks visiting and photographing new towns in Britain, the Netherlands, Sweden, Denmark, and Finland. Our happiness showed in the portraits taken by our next-door neighbor, a professional photographer.

6-9. Lallie in Tallahassee 1966

6-10. Dave in Tallahassee 1966

However, after the department chair recruited a psychologist with a PhD but no planning experience to a higher faculty rank than me, my hopes for the program's future were frustrated. It became clear that I would need a PhD to enjoy a satisfying academic career. I took leave in 1967, got an NDEA fellowship, gave up my USS English commanding officer's billet, and headed back to graduate school to enroll in a doctoral program. Harvard welcomed me, but wanted me to take economics courses; instead, I accepted Jack Parker's admission to the more land use-oriented UNC PhD program. Our life was about to enter another exciting new chapter as Lallie was pregnant.

6-11. Lallie 1967

7. THE NEW FAMILY BRANCH: 1967-2017

The big news of 1967 was the arrival in September of our son, David Kennedy Godschalk. Suddenly our lives expanded with the beginning of a lively new branch of the small Godschalk clan. David was actually born in the North Carolina Memorial Hospital, but we joked that he was born in a log cabin since we lived in a rental log cabin on Hillsborough Street at the time. After his baptism at the University Presbyterian Church, David got a new playmate in the form of Salty Dog, our new Beagle puppy. Fatherhood was a mystery to me, with more complexities to come.

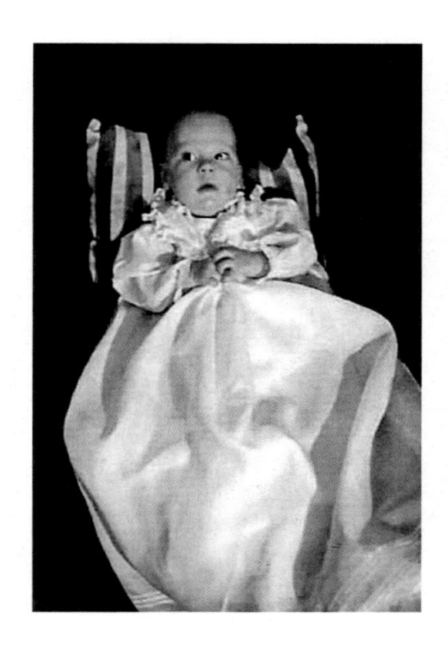

7-1. David Kennedy at Christening *7-2. Father and Son*

In 1969, we found a forested lot within a mile of campus and began to build a modern Deck House on the side of a hill facing Glendale Drive. However, construction slowed when our contractor began going bankrupt and checked himself into the mental wing at Duke Hospital. Meanwhile, we were evicted from the log cabin by our landlady who wanted to live there herself. She sent us a telegram on Christmas Eve, demanding that we move out immediately and raising our rent to $100 a day. Within a week, we moved, even though the new house was still under construction. When finally completed, the Deck House was a magnificent structure, with high ceilings, big window walls, mahogany trim, and cedar paneling. This would be David's home for the rest of his time in Chapel Hill. He found friends in the neighborhood and celebrated his birthdays on the deck. He attended local public schools and swam on the Tennis Club team.

7-3. Glendale Drive Deck House

In 1973, we spent a semester in Honolulu where I had a visiting appointment at the University of Hawaii. Even with a view of the sunset over Waikiki, six months of living on the 13th floor of a high-rise building convinced us that we needed to live closer to the earth. David attended Central Union preschool, as one of only two "haole" kids in his class. Lallies's mother came for an extended visit, joining us on weekend trips to the other islands, including Maui, Kauai, and the big island of Hawaii with its active volcano. We started snorkeling and watching the tropical fish on the Hawaiian reefs around the Islands. That would lead us to many future snorkeling trips, mostly on St. John, U.S. Virgin Islands.

Our favorite North Carolina vacation was to take one of our boats to the beach. We waterskied behind the Olé and sailed with our 15' O'Day Javelin in the sound behind the Bay House on Figure 8 Island. David and Lallie became qualified sailing skippers and we motored through the marsh with the centerboard up. Frequent man overboard drills made for fun ship handling. At one time, we were a three-boat family, when Lallie's mother contributed a fiberglass canoe to our fleet.

7-4. David Learns to Sail at Figure 8 Island 1976

Our family started cross-country skiing at the Trapp Family Lodge in Vermont. Although we did some downhill skiing, cross-country developed into another of our popular long-term recreational activities, first in Colorado and then in Montana. We found a congenial group of cross country skiers at Lone Mountain Ranch, a family-run lodge south of Bozeman, and went back for the spring season every year for 20 years, both with the kids, grandkids, friends, and by ourselves.

7-5. Cross Country Skiing *7-6. Lone Mountain Ranch 2003*

Lallie was a force in Chapel Hill organizations. She chaired the Horace Williams House Board and the Chapel Hill Library Board. She was clerk of course for swim meets at the Tennis Club while David was competing there. Her favorite activity was gardening. She turned our half-acre hillside into a manicured forest and wildflower sanctuary.

Travel took us from Chapel Hill out to far-flung cities and natural areas. We made two memorable trips to Alaska, hiking on the Kenai Peninsula and touring the coastal fiords by boat. We sailed on Lindblad Expedition boats in both the Caribbean Sea and Pacific Ocean. For my seventieth birthday, Lallie organized a special trip to Spain to enjoy the thrilling architecture and urban life in Barcelona and Bilbao. We immersed ourselves in Gaudi's Sagrada Familia and Gehry's Bilbao Guggenheim Museum. Despite not reading Catalan, Lallie navigated us smoothly through the cities, from the airports to the hotels and monuments.

Snorkeling gave us entre into the colorful underwater world. We tried several places in the Pacific, including Cabo San Lucas, but kept coming back to the Caribbean. Our favorite vacation spot was Gallows Point at St. John, U.S. Virgin Islands, where a great snorkeling reef was only about a hundred yards from our rental condominium and we could wander into Cruz Bay for drinks and dinner whenever we felt like it. On a good day, we might glimpse the elusive Spotted Drum, a pair of Eagle Rays, or a colorful octopus. Nothing like awakening to the toot of the morning ferry to remind you that life is good. If we felt like sampling other snorkeling spots, we could take off with Captain Sandy, the bikini-clad blond skipper of the Sadie Sea.

7-7. St. John USVI 2000 *7-8. Snorkeling, Cabo San Lucas 2006*

David grew into a handsome and adventuresome teenager. For his senior year in high school, he transferred to Deerfield Academy in Massachusetts. He then returned to Chapel Hill with a group of his friends to attend UNC, where he got his Bachelor's degree. He enjoyed a semester abroad in Italy, which led to extensive travel in Europe and the Middle East. We bought a house on Pritchard Avenue in the Northside neighborhood near down town, which became the home for David and his friends during their time at UNC, both during his undergraduate days and his subsequent return for a law degree. After renting it out for a couple of years, we donated it to UNC to establish the Godschalk Fellowship in Land Use and Environmental Planning.

7-9. David as Teenager with Lallie and Honey

David inherited the family love of travel. Following his graduation, he worked in London, trekked in the Himalayas, and decided to become a lawyer. After a year at the University of Colorado in Boulder, he finished his law degree at UNC. He worked as an attorney at HUD before entering the Master of Public Administration program at Harvard where the most significant event was not coursework but love. In Cambridge, he and Catherine Van Dusen, a fellow graduate student, met and fell in love. They announced their engagement on a trip to Europe, then graduated together and proceeded to her family house in Maine to marry.

Catherine and David's wedding in June 1999 was spectacular. Her Episcopal priest father, David Van Dusen, officiated at the ceremony in a meadow facing the Atlantic Ocean on Eggemoggin Reach with sailboats cruising in the background. Catherine came from a large and complex family, since both David and Althea, her father and mother, had children from previous marriages. The gracious and loving Althea welcomed us into the Van Dusen clan with open arms. Between family and friends, we entertained some 150 people at a pre-wedding lobster-bake picnic. My father-of-the-groom speech declaimed that robust connections were the key to both great architecture and enduring marriages and that love was the most powerful connector in the world. I joked that my own marriage rested on a "Lally column," an architectural term for a steel pipe filled with concrete that supports long-span beams.

7-10. Catherine and David's Wedding Maine 1999

After their honeymoon, Catherine and David settled into a historic town house on Dupont Circle in Washington, DC. He worked as a lawyer and she worked for Fannie Mae. Then in 2003 along came Peter Van Dusen Godschalk, our first grandchild. With his birth they headed to Montgomery County for more family-friendly housing, landing first in Chevy Chase and then in Bethesda within walking distance of Wood Acres Elementary School. Claire Rose Godschalk, Peter's sister, arrived in 2006, becoming the first girl born into the Godschalk family in over 100 years. Grandparenthood gave Lallie and me a brand new understanding of the joys of involvement with babies as they grow into distinct new young personalities.

7-11. Peter with Grandpa 2003

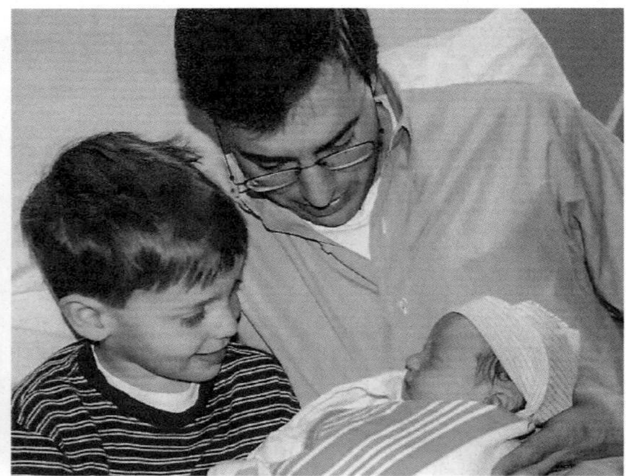

7-12. Claire, David, Peter 2006

Over the past 50 years, David and I have come to understand better each other's interests. In his job as general counsel in Alexandria for the Telesis Corporation (an inner city redevelopment firm), he now admits to the relevance of some of our dinner table discussions of zoning and urban design. Catherine also connects with my planning focus, in her work in Bethesda for the Calvert Foundation (a non-profit social impact investment organization). Catherine and David are spectacular parents. Our wonderful grandchildren are involved in an array of sports—swimming, soccer, lacrosse, basketball, baseball, and running, as well as music. Peter and I have connected over his Minecraft building projects and Lego models of Falling Water and other architectural icons. Claire and I have connected through our shared interest in painting and art. Freya, their white English Retriever, rounds out their household, which has included a series of German and Spanish *au pairs* over the years.

7-13. Peter and Claire with Device 2015

Relationships with our immediate family have been closest, but we have stayed in touch with other family members, including my father, stepmother, and brother. Dad died in 1983, following complications from a stroke. Roberta continued to live in the Enid house, with a life estate. She died in 2003, and Dick and I then sold the house. Before that, we took our sons, David and Mark, to Enid for a 'roots" trip to visit Roberta, look at the Cherokee Strip museum and our former family houses, and stay at the motel of Ray Davis, an old Enid friend. We looked in Marinus's garage but could not find the crosscut saw that cut the Rock Island railroad trestle.

7-14. Roots Trip Enid 2003. David, Roberta, and Mark

My brother Dick and I followed similar paths in early life. We both attended Dartmouth with NROTC fellowships and became naval officers. Then we took diverging paths. Where my instincts led me to adopt liberal values, Dick's instincts led him to adopt conservative values. He opted for a business career, going back to Dartmouth for an MBA degree after he finished his Navy active duty. In 1969, he married Pat Blohm and their son Mark was born the next year. He worked in international business development for many years, establishing overseas for-profit hospitals in Europe and the Middle East. In 1994, they retired in Macon, Georgia, where Dick does volunteer work. Pat has been captain of the Georgia state champion women's senior tennis team and is an expert Ichibana flower arranger. Mark, and his wife, Zenobia, and their sons, Chase and Finn, live in Atlanta, where both parents have successful business careers.

7-15. Dick, Mark, and Pat

The Navy also has remained a presence in my life. Continuing in the active Reserve with monthly drills and summer training duty, I served in a local Research Reserve unit linked with the naval office of underwater research. In 1979, the Naval Reserve promoted me to Commander in, and in 1980, I retired with pay after serving 20 years. The Navy extended the horizons of my life, providing unparalleled opportunities for service, leadership, responsibility, travel, and long-term friendships. Hearing "Anchors Away" played will always trigger a rich memory bank.

7-16. Commander Godschalk USNR

8. PROFESSING PLANNING: 1967-2004

At the same time as our new family branch was developing, my working days centered on the Department of City and Regional Planning at UNC. My roles over 37 fulfilling years with the Department went from PhD student and Lecturer at the start through the ranks to Emeritus Professor at the finish. The Department was an institutional sweet spot, providing me with brilliant teaching and research colleagues, freedom to pursue my own intellectual interests, and continuing organizational support.

Academic life at UNC was a natural for me. I entered the doctoral program in 1967 as a mature student with both teaching and practice experience. Within a year, the American Institute of Planners tapped me as editor of the *AIP Journal,* the planning profession's journal of record. That background helped me move directly into my dissertation on collaborative planning, conceived as a combination of design and consensus building and based on exploratory research in interviews with the residents and planners of the new towns of Columbia and Reston.

Completing my PhD in 1971, I accepted an offer from Jack Parker to join the UNC faculty at the Associate Professor level, rather than returning to FSU. My future academic career took root at UNC. I developed courses and research in participatory planning, dispute resolution, land use, site planning, growth management, hazard mitigation, and coastal planning. All of my work involved looking for ways to make planning more effective through design and consensus building.

8-1. Consensus Builder

In keeping with my tendency to bridge between fields, planning practice organizations recognized me with several honors. Stu Chapin and I were the first UNC planning faculty inducted as Fellows of the American Institute of Certified Planners (FAICP). As one of the only faculty members in my department with a background and continuing roots in planning practice, I was often at odds with my more theoretical colleagues. My standards for faculty recruiting and curriculum relevance differed from theirs. For example, I lobbied unsuccessfully for years to hire more urban designers and to replace the program's core course in microeconomics with a course in process skills and plan implementation, but my more theoretical colleagues out voted me.

8-2. AICP Fellows Award 1999

When civil rights leader Floyd McKissick proposed in 1969 to build Soul City, a free-standing, black-led new community in Warren County, I volunteered my planning services along with other UNC faculty. With planning funding from the U.S. Department of Housing and Urban Development, as one of the model new town projects under the Urban Growth and New Community Development Act, Soul City was located on a 5000-acre rural site north of Warrenton, North Carolina. Harvey Gant, fresh from his graduate planning degree program at MIT, became planning director; he and I taught a UNC course on new town planning, focused on Soul City. Conservative U.S. Senator Jesse Helms vehemently opposed the project, as did the Raleigh News and Observer, who assigned an investigative reporter to look for corruption. They did not find any, but succeeded in stirring up public sentiment against Soul City. Ultimately, a national economic downturn doomed the project by cancelling plans of manufacturing companies originally scheduled to open branch plants there. I hold great memories of working with Floyd and Harvey, though I still remember wondering at times if someone with a rifle was lurking in the woods outside our project meeting-place.

Whenever possible, I linked my teaching to actual planning events and processes. Since the most frequent U.S. planning conflicts focus on citizen fights against local growth and development, I designed a course on Development Dispute Resolution. Aware that dispute resolution skills could not be taught by lectures alone, I made the core of the course a series of increasingly complex role-play simulation exercises. Acting as public officials, developers, and neighborhood activists, students negotiated with each other to try to reach agreement, using a variety of consensus building techniques. We scored each exercise and based student grades on their relative scores and depth of post-exercise written analyses. Effectiveness depended on discovering the interests of the other parties, and achieving some measure of reciprocity. Former students reported that these skills were invaluable in their ensuing careers.

Most planning graduate students lacked design backgrounds, yet they needed to be able to grasp design principles and possibilities to be effective in planning practice. Students in my Site and Project Planning course were required to build three-dimensional models of their projects. The models, constructed of balsa wood and cardboard, depicted their proposed structures and roads laid out on the topographic contours and landscape of the site. (The cover photograph of this book shows an example.) By raising the designs up from the flat surface of the drawing page, the class was able to visualize more closely how their ideas might look if actually implemented. As new computer visualization programs, such as SketchUp with its advanced 3-D and rendering possibilities, became available, we switched to them. Studying these models often revealed potential new sweet spots.

Thanks to the writing skills and passion for ideas passed down from my father, I enjoyed a successful publishing and research career, with 12 professional books and a slew of journal articles. My focus was on linking planning practice and theory, and building tools for more effective professional work. UNC planning faculty such as Ed Kaiser, Stu Chapin, Phil Berke, Dave Brower, and Daniel Rodriguez were superb research colleagues and co-authors. Kaiser, Chapin, Berke, and I worked on land use planning. Brower and I worked on growth management and natural hazard mitigation. All of my 12 doctoral students graduated and some went on to become chairs and deans of planning schools and programs at places like the University of California at Irvine, Florida State University, Georgia Tech, Norfolk State University, and the University of Virginia. In 2002, the Association of Collegiate Schools of Planning honored me with their Distinguished Educator Award for lifetime contributions in teaching, service, education, and practice.

8-3. ACSP Distinguished Educator Award 2002

The University promoted me to department chair (where my model was the brilliant leadership of Jack Parker), then to full professor, and finally to holder of the Stephen Baxter Chaired Professorship. The Town elected me to a term on the Chapel Hill Town Council, where my growth management background was in demand. My comprehensive planning expertise supported my part-time consulting practice, advising on planning in Lee County, Florida, and acting as an expert witness in court cases defending plans in Sanibel, Florida, and other places. The Business School appointed me as adjunct professor to teach site planning and project planning to real estate MBA students for a couple of years.

8-4. Town Council Swearing-In 1985

Within the University, I chaired the Chancellor's buildings and grounds committee and worked with the consultants on developing the 2001 UNC master plan. The department history described me as perhaps "the most highly respected and best-known face of DCRP for four decades." My phased retirement began in 2001 and I formally retired in 2004, continuing to lecture and teach one course a year for several years.

Two co-authored books have been among my most widely read publications. I joined with Ed Kaiser and Stu Chapin to write the fourth edition of *Urban Land Use Planning* (University of Illinois Press) and then continued with Ed, Phil Berke, and Daniel Rodriguez on the fifth edition of this popular textbook. My book, *Natural Hazard Mitigation* (Island Press) is an influential analysis and set of recommendations to improve policies for reducing impacts of floods, hurricanes, and other disasters, written with a group of colleagues and research assistants with funding from a National Science Foundation research grant. My most widely cited journal article, "Urban Hazard Mitigation: Creating Resilient Cities," was published in the wake of the 9/11 bombing of the World Trade Center in *Natural Hazards Review* (2003).

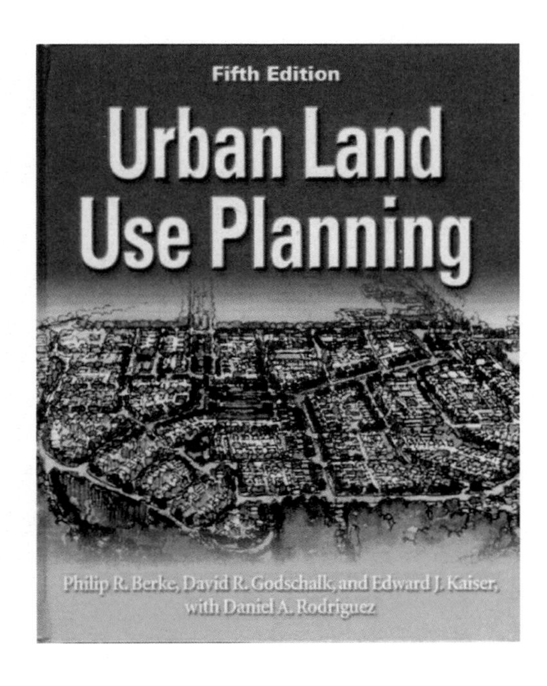

8-5. Urban Land Use Planning

8-6. Natural Hazard Mitigation

To give back to the Department of City and Regional Planning, which had supported my professional life for some fifty years, Lallie and I created the Godschalk Fellowship in Land Use and Environmental Planning within the UNC College of Arts and Sciences. To fund the Fellowship, we donated our two/thirds interest in the 209 Pritchard Avenue house where David had lived during his university years. To mark the gift, the University photographed us in front of the aerial photo-mural of historic New York City in the entry to New East Building, home of the planning program.

8-7. Recognition of Godschalk Fellowship

9. RETIREMENT AT CAROL WOODS: 2008-2017

Lallie and I now live at Carol Woods, a 500-resident continuing care retirement community in Chapel Hill, in a wooded 125-acre site. This is a unique place where residents are deeply involved in community life, activities, and decision-making. It was hard to give up our beautiful Deck House and wooded hillside garden, but I believe moving here in 2008 was one of the best and most well timed moves of my life.

In spring 2008, we sold our Glendale Drive Deck House and two nearby houses that we rented out and moved to a duplex cottage on the Lower Loop in Carol Woods. We knew the community well. Lallie's mother lived here for the final 13 years of her life, until her death in 1993. I served on the Carol Woods Board, led by Pat Sprig, the astute CEO, who asked me to chair their Master Plan Task Force, which would prepare plans for major new additions to the library, fitness center, apartments, and other facilities. The Task Force consisted of a selected group of residents, members of the Carol Woods Board, and senior staff.

Preparing the Master Plan was a challenging exercise in design and consensus building. From 2006 to 2010, the Task Force worked with a team of design consultants led by architect, Robert Sotolongo, and landscape architect, Dan Jewel, to analyze the suggestions from resident meetings and focus groups and a resident survey. We needed to ensure that Carol Woods remains attractive to current and future markets, affordable, and financially solvent, and delivers high quality service to a diverse resident population for generations to come. Our starting point was a long list of resident and staff proposals for new facilities and spaces. Gradually we identified the key needs and tested various schemes for realizing them.

9-1. Carol Woods Master Plan Task Force. Left to right: Jim Call, Director; Pat Sprig, CEO; Dave Godschalk, Chair and Board member; Bill Koch, resident; Jon Howes, former Board chair; Dave Wilkerson, VP Operations; Mary Ann Gross, resident; Caroline Sikorsky, resident. Not pictured: Mary Beck, Board member; and John Hawkins, Board member.

Carol Woods' residents reviewed and commented on all Master Plan schemes. It was relatively easy to get agreement on proposed new amenities, such as a fitness center, library and art room expansion, and craft building enlargement, as well as a new main entry portal, a new elevator, and some interior improvements. However, adding new residential units was controversial, even though the land was available and the demand was high. Current residents objected to adding to the campus population and they considered the available sites for new town houses to be too far from the center of the community. In response, the Task Force proposed adding new apartment units to an existing central residential building. When residents learned the revenue from the eighteen new apartments would balance the costs of the new amenities so that their monthly fees would not increase, the objections quieted. Finding the Master Plan sweet spot required discovering the right balance between current resident interests and future community needs.

Lallie and I had fun remodeling our unit, particularly adding a screen porch with a view of the woods behind. Neighbors who arrived with us formed a "Class of 2008" contingent and hold annual alumni dinners. The class remains intact in 2017, with the exception of Foster Owen who died in 2014

9-2. Class of 2008 Dinner 2011. Left to right: Jerry and Linda Folda, Dave and Lallie Godschalk, Dan and Linda Textoris, David and Betty Hughes, Foster and Jean Owen.

Sadly, Casey, our cherished Golden Retriever, did not live long after our move. She was the last of our canine line. Salty Dog, our irrepressible Beagle, was the first, growing up from puppyhood in the playpen with son David. Frosty, our magnificent Husky, was the second, leading us a merry chase from places like the girls' dorm at Carolina at midnight to the far reaches of Orange County. We miss these faithful companions, but without a fenced yard, we are no longer up to the demands of keeping a dog.

9-3. Casey at Dog Park

Lallie's skills at gardening and library work are much in demand at Carol Woods. In short order, she became chair of the Gardens and Landscape Committee, charged with handling the re-landscaping needed to adapt to the new construction under the Master Plan. She also joined the Library Committee and took charge of buying new books and dealing with contributed materials. Her committees are famous for getting results without bureaucratic delays.

My professional books and articles have always focused on understanding how planning works in practice and on building tools to make that practice more effective. At Carol Woods, I write regular book reviews for *Urban Land Magazine*. The American Planning Association asked me to chair a task force to set new sustainability standards for comprehensive plans. That work culminated in two APA reports and a plan certification program, for which I received the 2015 APA President's Award in recognition of distinguished contributions in advancing the planning profession.

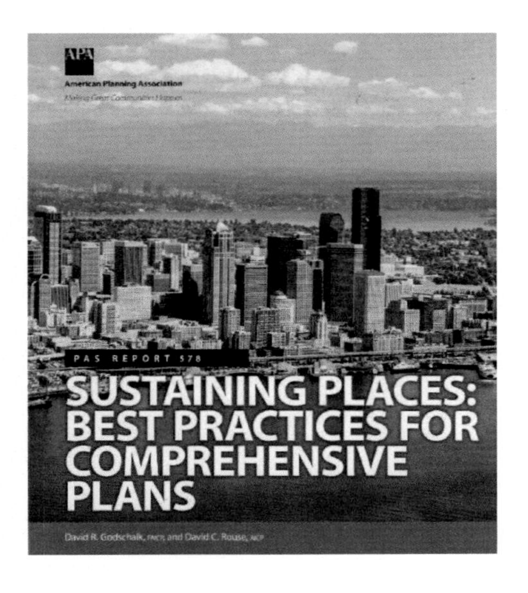

9-4. Sustaining Places Report

Another writing project that I finished at Carol Woods was a history of the build-out of the ambitious UNC 2001 master plan. After playing leadership roles in this ten-year process, Jon Howes (a planning colleague, former Chapel Hill Mayor, and Carol Woods' resident) and I decided to publish a book about it. Using our notes and memories, along with University sources, we wrote *The Dynamic Decade: Creating the Sustainable Campus for the University of North Carolina at Chapel Hill 2001-2011*. To capture the scope of the transformation for the book's cover, Jon and I flew over campus in a helicopter with an aerial photographer.

9-5. The Dynamic Decade *9-6. Dave and Jon with Helicopter*

This account contains many sweet spots, most related to the implementation of the plan's transformative vision against daunting institutional and political odds. Rarely is a university able to bring together the players, designs, and resources to move itself this far ahead in this short a period. In one ten year span, six million square feet of new buildings were constructed; a million square feet renovated; and five million square feet of pedestrian paths and open space created. To enable this leap forward, a new zoning category was devised that required approval of a ten-year development plan by the Town, overcoming the delays imposed by the previous special use permit process.

Retirement has enabled me to explore my sensuous side. I had dabbled with watercolor painting before we moved, but found the time and facilities to carry it forward at Carol Woods. The art studio with lots of fellow artists is just a block from our house. Before long, painting had become one of my daily activities, paired with writing as a happy alternation between right and left-brain projects. I have indulged myself with watercolor courses from the Carrboro Art Center, Durham Arts Council, Cheap Joes in Boone, and plein air painting workshops in Venice Beach in 2015, and New York City and New Orleans in 2016. I also have done portraits of my grandchildren, Peter and Claire, my great friend, Fred Chase, as well as Robert Frost, the poet whose reading introduced me to my future wife, and our memorable Lone Mountain Ranch folk singer, Bruce Anfinson.

9-7. Madison Avenue Watercolor 2016

Happily, I have been able to keep my hand in professional design work. As a member of the UNC Design Review Group, I participate in regular assessments of all campus architecture and construction projects. As a member of the Orange County Habitat for Humanity Site Committee, I work with a group of real estate and design professionals on land acquisition and site planning for affordable housing projects. As an occasional part-time consultant with Clarion Associates, I enjoy involvement in comprehensive planning project assignments with Ben Herman, Roger Waldon, Craig Richardson, and others.

Rachel Kaplan describes "restorative landscapes" as ones that hit "the sweet spot" of being interesting, enticing, aesthetic, and a little mysterious (quoted in F. Williams, *The Nature Fix*, Norton, 2017). Lallie and I continue to look for restorative landscapes in both developed places like Rome, Berlin, Havana, Costa Rica, and Iceland, as well as in islands, shorelines, national parks, coastal Maine, and other destinations. Often I paint a landscape scene from our travels as a memory sketch.

Aging has brought a deeper understanding of who we are and who we have been. It has meant saying good-bye to many special people, including our parents, mentors, and closest friends. It has meant facing up to necessary endings of favorite activities, like teaching, skiing, and tennis. And it has meant realizing that some of life's most wrenching disruptions, like being recalled to active Navy duty during the Berlin Crisis and being abandoned by political supporters in Gainesville, have turned out to be good things in the end, pushing us to adapt to new and better life pursuits. Above all, it has shown us how lucky we have been to have each other as companions as we walk into the future.

9-8. Walking Together

Our eighth decade is different from our earlier times but still engaging. We have become opera buffs, thanks to the Metropolitan Opera's High Definition broadcasts at the local theater. Our family keeps us in touch with the changing social and cultural worlds, and the challenges of coming of age in the twenty-first century. Our retirement community provides continuing physical and communal support, as well as satisfying outlets for our talents. Our marriage remains the bedrock and sweetest spot of our emotional life.

APPENDX. FAMILLY TREE; RESUMÉ

The backstory of this memoir includes both the family antecedents, as shown in my family tree, and a brief listing of activities that engaged me during my professional life, as shown in my resumé.

This family tree diagram shows the people and relationships of my branch of the Godschalk family. The memoir does not discuss all of the people because it focuses on those closest to me, but they are all part of my family story. Its preparation was a labor of love by Jort Okhuijzen, the son of my Dutch second cousin Vera and her husband Johannes. He found that our early ancestors were German and moved to Norg in the Netherlands in the early 18th century, changing their name from Gottschalk to the Dutch Godschalk. Bertha told me that the name might mean either God's Marshall or God's Jester.

A-1. Jort and Dave 2015

Jort has traced the Godschalk family back through eight generations to Jacob Samuels Godschalk. Jacob was born in Schüttorf, Germany, in 1766; he married Margje Mozes; and he died in Norg, Netherlands, in 1832. The parents of my grandfather, Marinus Godschalk, were Jacob Godschalk, who was born in Norg and died in Assen, Netherlands, and Sara Meibergen, who was born in Almelo and died in Assen, where the family owned a brush factory for many years. The family suffered greatly during the Nazi occupation of the Netherlands in World War II: 64 died in concentration camps.

My middle name is Robinson, after my mother's family. Mother's cousin, Thelma West Smith Elliott, has compiled information on the Robinson branch of the family. Mother's parents moved to Enid from Tennessee. Her father, Oscar, was one of eleven children born to James and Samantha Robinson in the late 1800's, and her mother, Nannie, was one of six children born to James Parker Barry and Tennessee Helen West during that time.

Tennessee was a border state during the Civil War. James Parker, Barry twelve at the time of the war, was man of the house from when his father joined the Confederate army until his father deserted to come back and take care of them. While he was away in service, passing Union troops confiscated all of their food and farm animals. The Barry family had no slaves.

The West family migrated to Tennessee from Delaware, where possibly (records are inconclusive) "our" Thomas West was also Baron De La Warre, appointed by the Crown as the first Governor of Virginia in 1609. Around 1804, Thomas West came into Tennessee with several other families, all bringing their slaves with them. He purchased the land that became the family household location for several generations.

Before Nannie and Oscar moved to Oklahoma Territory, other relatives also moved there. Felix West's wife, Lulu Shockley, was 1/8th Choctaw Indian, and they moved to Ardmore in hopes of receiving tribal land. Later on, Nannie's father, Gipson West, moved to Ardmore around 1907, where he lived into his ninety's.

Because the Godschalk and Robinson ancestors had many children, and documentation is sometimes scarce, this account touches only a few high spots of the much larger and more complex family tree.

Our Grandparents' Generation: Marinus, Bertha, Oscar, Nannie

Our Parents' Generation: Roberta, Harold, Helen

Our Generation: Lallie, Dave, Dick, Pat

Our Children's Generation: David, Catherine, Mark, Zenobia

Our Grandchildren's Generation: Peter, Claire, Chase, Finn

RESUMÉ
Dr. David R. Godschalk FAICP

Emeritus Professor of Planning, Department of City and Regional Planning
University of North Carolina, Chapel Hill, NC

EDUCATION

1971 Ph.D. (Planning), University of North Carolina, Chapel Hill, NC. NDEA Fellow

1964 M.R.P. (Regional Planning), University of North Carolina, Chapel Hill, NC. Pittsburgh Plate Glass Foundation Fellow. Student Award, AIP.

1959 B. Arch. (Architecture), University of Florida, Gainesville, FL with honors. Phi Kappa Phi, Gargoyle Honorary Society, Florida Association of Architects Medal, Alpha Rho Chi Medal.

1953 B.A. (Modified Art), Dartmouth College, Hanover, NH. Magna Cum Laude. NROTC Regular Scholarship. Phi Beta Kappa.

EMPLOYMENT

Professor Emeritus: Dept. of City and Regional Planning, UNC, Chapel Hill, 2004--present.

Stephen Baxter Professor (University endowed chair): UNC, Chapel Hill, 1994-2004.

Chair: Dept. of City and Regional Planning, UNC, Chapel Hill, 1978-1983.

Professor: Dept. of City and Regional Planning, UNC, Chapel Hill, 1977-2004.

Scholar in Residence: Southern Growth Policies Board, Research Triangle Park, NC, 1977-1978.

Visiting Associate Professor: Pacific Urban Studies & Planning, University of Hawaii, Honolulu, 1973.

Associate Professor: Dept. of City and Regional Planning, UNC, Chapel Hill, 1972-1977.

Lecturer: Dept. of City and Regional Planning, UNC, Chapel Hill, 1969-1971.

Editor: *Journal of the American Institute of Planners*, 1968-1971.

Assistant Professor: Dept. of Urban & Regional Planning, Florida State University, Tallahassee, 1965-67.

Planning Director: City of Gainesville, Florida, 1964-1965.

Vice President: Milo Smith Associates, Planning Consultants, Tampa, Florida, 1959-1961.

MILITARY SERVICE

U.S. Navy, Active Sea Duty, 1953-1956 and 1961-1962 (Berlin Crisis recall). CDR, USNR (Retired)

PUBLIC SERVICE

Orange County Habitat for Humanity, Advisory Board and Site Planning Committee, 2007--present. Charrette facilitator and design advisor, Sunrise Road community plan, 2004-2006.

North Carolina Botanical Garden Foundation, Board of Directors, 2003-2007.

Governor's appointee, North Carolina Commission to Address Smart Growth, Growth Management, and Development Issues, 2000-2001.

UNC/Chapel Hill Outlying Campus Zoning District Ordinance Committee, 1996-1997.

Sustainable Cities Symposium, Steering Committee Member and Work Group Leader, Research Triangle Park, NC, 1996.

Orange Water and Sewer Authority, Cane Creek Watershed Advisory Committee. 1994-1997.

North Carolina Legislative Research Commission: Study Committee on Statewide Comprehensive Planning, 1991-1993.

Director, Peer Review, Fixed Guideway Study, Triangle Transit Authority, 1992.

Member, Town Council, Chapel Hill, NC, April-December, 1985 (Appointed); December, 1985-November, 1989 (Elected).

Negotiating Team, Joint Planning Agreement and University Lake Watershed (Chapel Hill, Carrboro, and Orange County, NC) 1986-89

NC AIA Urban Design Assistance Team, *Riverfront Plan*, Asheville, NC, April 26-29, 1989.

Chair, Task Force on Growth Management, Town of Chapel Hill, NC, Fall, 1984.

Member, Energy, Environment and Natural Resources Committee, NC League of Municipalities, 1986-88.

Vice Chair, Land Use Advisory Committee, Triangle J Council of Governments, 1987-1988.

Warren Regional Planning Corporation (Soul City), North Carolina: Secretary, 1970-76; Board of Directors, 1970-78.

CERTIFICATIONS

Fellow, American Institute of Certified Planners. (FAICP).

Registered Architect (Inactive), State of Florida.

Made in the USA
Middletown, DE
04 May 2017